Table of Contents

32. Holiday Mimosa
33. Holly   Berry
34.   Jack   Frost   Martini
35.   Kandy   Kane
36. La Vie En Rouge (Life in Red)
37. Merry Christi
38. Merry Christmas
39. Merry Irishman
40. Mistletoe Aperitif
41. Mistletoe   Martini
42. Peach Pomegranate Holiday Martini
43. Poinsettia
44. Pumpkin Pie Cocktail
45. Pumpkin Spice Martini
46. Red Night
47. Red Rocket
48. Reindeer Caesar
49. Santa   Shot
50. Scotch Holiday Sour
51. Scroogedriver
52. Snowball
53. Snow Job
54. Tezon   Misteltoe
55. White Christmas #1
56. White Christmas #2
57. White Christmas Dream
58. White Russian
59. Winter Breeze
60. Winter Ice
61. Winter   Sun

Go Nog Their Socks Off

1. Baltimore Eggnog
2. Bourbon Eggnog
3. Brandy Eggnog
4. California   Eggnog
5. Christmas Cheer Eggnog
6. Cider Nog (Non-alcoholic)

'Tis The Season To Be Jolly

Christmas is coming, as well as it's the period to be jolly!
The holiday is a favorite duration for a lot of us. You'll notice events as
well as happenings all over us bringing the spirit of the time of year out
in everybody.
When you'll be tossing an event on your own, it's that period of year.
This year, you can easily make that get together added jolly and
remarkable. You can extend the cheery sprightliness to the alcoholic
drinks and also beverages you offer your party guests.
You will find a number of incredible drinks fitting the holiday mood
perfectly which you can use. The fascinating and delightful drink dishes
accumulated below permit you a head start. From Angel's Delight to
Winter Sun, you're sure to discover some mixed drinks to your taste.
Let's drink to Happy Holidays!

1. Angel's Delight

Ingredients

1oz cream
3/4 oz three-way sec 3/4 oz gin
2-3 dashboards grenadine

Offers 1

Guidelines

Shake all ingredients well in a cocktail shaker with ice. Strain right into

a chilled cocktail glass for serving.

2. Angel's Wing

Components
1/2 oz crème de cacao
1/2 oz brandy 1 tablespoon cream

Serves 1

Directions
Layer the components as complies with: crème de cacao (white), brandy
(brown), cream (white). Serve in Pousse Cafe glass or specialized glass.

3. Black Santa

Components

3/4 oz Liqueur, coffee (Kahlua) 1/2 oz Vodka
1/4 oz Schnapps, pepper mint Serves 1

Directions

Load half an antique glass with ice. Put coffee liqueur and also

vodka right into glass. Include peppermint schnapps to serve.

4. Blue Snowflake

Ingredients

2oz Hpnotiq
1 dash Vodka
1 oz Pineapple Juice Serves 1

Directions

Shake and also blend all ingredients plus ice in a cocktail shaker. Pressure into

cocktail glass.

5. Brandy Frost
Ingredients

2 oz milk (or half-and-half cream) 1/2 oz white crème de cacao

1 oz brandy
1 tbsp peppermint schnapps candy walking stick
Serves 1

Guidelines

Mix all liquid ingredients well in a cocktail shaker with ice. Pressure
right into a.

cocktail glass. Garnish with candy cane to offer.

6. Sweet Cane.

Ingredients.

3/4 oz Peppermint Schnapps 3/4 oz SKYY Berry vodka 3/4 oz white
Crème de Cacao 1/4 oz grenadine.
pepper mint sweet, crushed half-and-half.
7-Up.

Serves 1.

Instructions

Put ice in cocktail shaker. Add in peppermint Schnapps, SKYY Berry.

vodka, white Creme de Cacao, and also grenadine. Shake well. Rim
alcoholic drink glass with smashed pepper mint sweet, after that gather
the mix. Full of half-and-half. Top with a dash of 7-Up to offer.

7. Candy Cane Martini.

Ingredients.

1.5 oz vodka.
1 tsp pepper mint schnapps.

1 little candy walking stick Serves 1.

Instructions

Shake vodka and also peppermint schnapps with ice in a cocktail shaker.

Stress into a chilled cocktail glass. Garnish with a little candy walking stick to serve.

8. Christmas Bellringer.

Ingredients.

1 tsp triple sec (eg. Cointreau).
1.5 oz gin.
0.75 oz liquore Gaetano.
0.5 oz lemon Juice.
0.75 oz orange Juice 1 twist orange.
Serves 1.

Instructions

Shake all fluid active ingredients in cocktail shaker with ice. Strain right into.

cocktail glass. Press twist before a lantern fire to launch a flaming ruptured of oil right into drink, as well as throw spin in to serve.

9. Xmas Cheer.

Ingredients.

1 passionfruit, juiced 1 oz peach schnapps 1 oz vodka.
1 mug chilled cranberry juice 1/2 cup ice.
Offers 2.

Instructions

Shake all active ingredients in a cocktail shaker well. Pressure right into 2 glasses to offer.

10. Xmas Cosmopolitan.

Ingredients.

1/2 oz Cointreau.
1/2 oz cranberry juice 1 tsp lime juice, fresh 1 oz vodka cranberries.
Serves 1.

Instructions

Mix all liquid ingredients well in a shaker with ice. Pressure into a
cooled.

liqueur glass. Float a couple of cranberries to garnish.

11. Christmas In A Cup.

Ingredients.

1 oz After Shock 1 oz Rum, spiced 2 oz Dr. Pepper.
Offers 1.

Instructions

Put Dr. Pepper and also rum in a beer cup as well as mix. Include After
Shock in and.

let it blend on its own.

12. Xmas In Mexico.

Ingredients.

3 shots tequila, gold 3/4 pint cranberry juice.

3 dashes grenadine 2 dashes sour mix 1 slice lime.
6 whole cranberries.

Offers 1.

Instructions

Integrate as well as drink all liquid components plus ice in a cocktail shaker.

Pressure right into highball glass. Garnish with cranberries and lime. Optionally include salt.

13. Xmas Martini.

Ingredients.

3 oz cranberry mixed drink or raspberry alcoholic drink 1/2 oz crème de cassis.
1 oz vodka.

Offers 1.

Instructions

Shake all components in cocktail shaker with ice. Strain into a cooled.

liqueur glass to offer.

14. Christmas Pudding.

Ingredients.

1 oz Drambuie.
5 oz Stout (Guinness) 1 oz Southern Comfort.
Serves 1.

Instructions

Mix ingredients in a shaker and also stress right into a red wine glass.

15. Cola De Mono (Monkey's Tail).
Components 6 cups milk.
1 mug sugar.
1tsp ground cinnamon 1/4 mug immediate coffee.
2cups Chilean aguardiente (eg. cachaça, rhum, grappa, tequila, vodka,

Doppelkorn).
1 tsp vanilla extract Serves 12.

Instructions.

Mix the milk, sugar, and cinnamon together and also slowly offer steam for.

3minutes.
Dissolve the coffee as well as include in the combination. Awesome and placed it in the fridge. When cold, include the aguardiente. Pour into capped containers and refrigerate additionally up until chilled. This mix can keep in the fridge for 2 weeks till required.
Offer really cold.

16. Depaz Winter Mojito.

Ingredients.

0.25 oz fresh lime juice.
1.5 oz Depaz Cane Syrup.
1.75 oz Depaz Blue Cane Amber Rhum 6-8 cranberries.
8-10 mint leaves icing sugar.
Offers 1.

Instructions

Put all liquid components in cocktail shaker. Put in ice, and also half or more.

of the cranberries and mint leaves. Shake intensely to break open the cranberries during the drinking. Stress into ice-filled highball glass. Include continuing to be cranberries. Garnish with a mint sprig, finishing its top with topping sugar.

17. Desiring for Zen.

Ingredients.

1oz Zen Green Tea Liqueur 1/2 oz Midori Melon Liqueur 3 oz mango

juice.
2oz cream white pepper mint leaves grated nutmeg.
Serves 1.

Instructions

Shake all fluid ingredients, white pepper, plus ice in cocktail shaker.

well. Stress right into Champagne flute. Top with mint leaves and also nutmeg to garnish.

18. Pet dog Sled.

Ingredients.

1.5 oz Canadian whisky.
1.5 oz orange juice 1 tsp grenadine.
1 tablespoon lemon juice Serves 1.

Instructions

Shake all components in cocktail shaker with ice or blend in blender.

Stress into chilled Old Fashioned glass to serve.

19. Down Under Snowball.

Ingredients.

1 oz Rum, light.
1oz Schnapps, peach.
0.5 oz Grenadine 3 oz Orange Juice.
Offers 1.

Instructions

Blend all active ingredients in a blender with ice. Pressure into a coupette glass.

for serving.

20. Fir Tree Shot.

Ingredients.

1/2 oz environment-friendly pepper mint schnapps 1/2 oz grenadine.
1/3 oz Baileys Irish Cream Serves 1.

Instructions.

Layer the liquids in a shot glass beginning with Baileys Irish Cream.

(white), then grenadine (red), and also top by pepper mint schnapps (environment-friendly). When adding the 3rd and also 2nd layer to aid stay clear of the blending of the fluids, put over the back of a tsp very carefully.

21. Fontana Christmas Crantini.

Ingredients.

1.5 oz Liqueur, orange 1 oz Vodka.
2oz Cranberry Juice 1 Orange slice.

Offers 1.

Instructions

Shake all fluid active ingredients well in a cocktail shaker with ice. Stress right into.

a huge liqueur glass. Leading with a rounded orange piece as garnish.

22. Frostbite.

Ingredients.

1.5 oz tequila.
0.5 oz white crème de cacao.
0.5 oz blue curaçao.

0.5 oz cream.
1 maraschino cherry for garnish Serves 1.

Instructions

Shake all ingredients well with ice in a cocktail shaker. Pressure right into a.

cooled mixed drink glass or serve in antique glass on the rocks. Leading with maraschino cherry for garnish.

23. Frosty Fizz.

Ingredients.

8 oz pomegranate juice 8 clementines, juiced.
3 tbsp sugar.
1 oz Grand Marnier.
25.5 oz Prosecco Serves 6.

Instructions

Layer the sugar uniformly over a little plate or dish. Prepare 6 glasses.

and also cut one clementine in half. Massage the rim of each glass with the cut clementine prior to dipping in the plate/saucer for a coat of sugar.

Juice the continuing to be clementines and mix well with pomegranate juice and liqueur. Pour the blend into the 6 glasses prepared earlier and also top with Prosecco.

24. G'ingle Bell.

Ingredients.

1 oz G'vine Nouaison.
0.25 oz Lillet Blanc.
0.5 oz apple liqueur (Berentzen).
0.5 oz easy syrup.
0.25 oz lime juice Serves 1.

Instructions.

Shake all components well in a cocktail shaker before straining into a.

alcoholic drink glass.

25. G'vine Frost Bite.

Ingredients.

1.5 oz G'vine Gin.
1tsp lemon pepper zest.
1.5 oz Averna limoncello Serves 1.

Instructions.

Mix ice along with all active ingredients well.

26. Gingerbread Apple Cocktail.

Ingredients.

2oz Domaine de Canton 1 oz vanilla vodka.

2.5 oz apple cider.
A few declines of lemon juice Orange zest.
Agave syrup Serves 1.

Instructions

Line a cooled martini glass gently with agave syrup. Shake all liquid.

components in a cocktail shaker, after that stress right into glass. Grate orange zest to serve.

27. Gingerbread Man.

Ingredients.

1 oz Bailey's Irish Cream 1 oz Goldschläger.
1oz Schnapps, butterscotch 1 oz Vodka.
Offers 1.

Instructions.

Mix all ingredients with ice in a cocktail shaker. Pressure right into shot glass.

28. Grinch.

Ingredients.

2oz Midori.
1/2 oz lemon juice, fresh 1 tsp sugar syrup.
1 red cherry.

Offers 1.

Instructions.

Shake all ingredients with ice in a cocktail shaker. Pressure right into a chilled.

mixed drink or liqueur glass. Top with cherry to offer.

29. Happy Holly-Daze.

Ingredients.

1 oz Bailey's Irish Cream 1 oz Kahlua.
0.5 oz Rum, spiced.
0.5 oz Schnapps, peppermint.
1.5 oz Milk Serves 1.

Instructions.

Pour all active ingredients into a cocktail shaker. Add ice. Shake well prior to.

stressing right into glass.

30. Incredible Christmas Jones.

Ingredients.

5 oz pineapple juice 1 part vodka.
4 fresh strawberries 2 tsp superfine sugar 7-Up or Sprite.
mint sprig Serves 2.

Instructions

Blend the pineapple juice, vodka, strawberries, and also sugar with each other.

Strain right into highball glasses as well as top with 7-Up or Sprite. Garnish with mint sprig.

31. Vacation Hopper.

Ingredients.

1 oz Midori melon liqueur 1/2 oz eco-friendly creme de menthe 1/2 oz white creme de cacao 2 oz half-and-half.
mint leaves raspberry.
Serves 1.

Instructions

Shake all fluid active ingredients in a cocktail shaker well with ice. Strain right into.

a cocktail glass. Garnish with mint leaves and also raspberry to serve.

32. Vacation Mimosa.

Ingredients.

1/4 mug orange liqueur (eg. Grand Marnier) 2 tablespoon white sugar.
1 cup orange juice.
1 container (25 oz) brut sparkling wine, chilled Serves 6.

Instructions

Put several of the orange liqueur in a superficial dish, and also load a saucer with.

the sugar. Prepare 6 alcoholic drink glasses. Dip the edge of each first in the orange liqueur, then in the sugar for a thin sugar coat.
Load the 6 glasses evenly with orange juice as well as continuing to be orange liqueur.
Top with champagne to serve.

33. Holly Berry.

Ingredients.

1.5 oz Plymouth Gin.
0.125 oz lemon juice, fresh raspberry juice.

fresh raspberries Serves 1.

Instructions

Shake Plymounth Gin, and also fresh lemon juice in a cocktail shaker with.

ice. Pressure into a mixed drink glass. Fill glass up with raspberry juice. Leading with fresh raspberries to garnish.

34. Jack Frost Martini.

Ingredients.

1.5 oz vodka Peppermint schnapps Peppermint candy stick.
Serves 1.

Instructions

Stir vodka with a float of pepper mint schnapps over ice. Stress and.

garnish with a pepper mint candy cane.

35. Kandy Kane.

Ingredients.

1oz crème de noyaux 1 oz Rumble Minze.
Serves 1.

Instructions

Layer Creme de Noyaux over Rumple Minze to offer.

36. La Vie En Rouge (Life in Red).

Ingredients.

fresh rosemary needles.
0.5 oz basic syrup.

1.5 oz Grand Marnier.
1.5 oz cranberry juice, fresh.
0.5 oz lemon juice, fresh rosemary sprig.
Offers 1.

Instructions

Mash 10-12 rosemary needles gently with basic syrup in an alcoholic drink.

shaker. Pour in the other fluid **Ingredients.** Include ice and drink well. Pressure into a rocks glass with ice. Drift rosemary sprig to serve.

37. Merry Christi.

Ingredients.

2.5 oz Christiana vodka.
2.5 oz milk.
2tbsp hot chocolate mix Serves 1.

Instructions

Mix ingredients together and also garnish with dark delicious chocolate shavings.

38. Merry Christmas.

Ingredients.

1oz Plymouth Gin 1 oz cranberry juice 1 tsp lemon juice club soda. fresh or dried cranberries Serves 1.

Instructions.

Load ice in a collins glass. Add in gin, cranberry juice and also lemon juice.

and also mix. Top with club soda. Garnish with cranberries.

39. Merry Irishman.

Ingredients.

2oz Tullamore Dew Irish Whiskey 1 oz Kahlua.
1/2 oz mint schnapps sweet cane.
Serves 1.

Instructions

Pour all alcohol components in an iced-filled rocks glass. Garnish and also mix.

with sweet cane.

40. Mistletoe Aperitif.

Ingredients.

1/2 oz Chambord.
1/2 oz melon liqueur (Midori) 1/2 oz Orange liqueur.
Serves 1.

Instructions.

Layer the liqueur in a high shot glass in this order: Chambord, melon.

liqueur, orange liqueur. (Tip: Pour over the rear of a spoon to normal the flows on top without blending.) Flambe for a couple of secs making certain the glass has cooled down before alcohol consumption.

41. Mistletoe Martini.

Ingredients.

3oz cooled cranberry natural tea 2 oz orange juice.
2 oz vodka.

3/4 oz lemon juice 3 tsp sugar.
Offers 2.

Instructions.

Shake all components in a cocktail shaker well with ice. Pressure into.

martini glasses to serve.

42. Peach Pomegranate Holiday Martini.

Ingredients.

1 oz Van Gogh Pomegranate Vodka 3/4 oz Peach Schnapps.
1 oz orange juice dash of lemon juice ground cinnamon granulated sugar.
Serves 1.

Instructions

Mix all liquid ingredients in a cocktail shaker well with ice. Strain right into.

cooled alcoholic drink glass. Sprinkle cinnamon as well as sugar on the top to offer.

43. Poinsettia.

Ingredients.

4 oz brut Champagne.
1.5 tbsp cranberry juice Serves 1.

Instructions.

Cool all components beforehand. Load champagne groove with sparkling wine.

Gather cranberry juice to offer.

44. Pumpkin Pie Cocktail.

Ingredients.

2 scoops vanilla ice cream 1/2 cup crushed ice.
1 tbsp tinned pumpkin.
1 oz half-and-half or light cream 1 oz spiced rum.
1/4 tsp pumpkin pie spice 2 tablespoon whipped topping.
1 pinch pumpkin pie seasoning Serves 1.

Instructions

Blend gelato, ice, pumpkin, cream or half-and-half, rum, as well as 1/4 tsp.

pumpkin pie spice till smooth. Pour into glass, add whipped topping, and also sprinkle with pinch of pumpkin pie seasoning to serve.

45. Pumpkin Spice Martini.

Ingredients.

1 jigger (1.5 oz) vanilla flavorful vodka (eg. Stoli) 1 jigger (1.5 oz) Irish cream liqueur (eg. Bailey's).
1 jigger (1.5 oz) pumpkin flavored liqueur (eg. Hiram Walker) 1 cup ice.
1 pinch ground cinnamon 1 pinch ground nutmeg.
Offers 1.

Instructions

Shake all liqueur ingredients in cocktail shaker plus ice cubes. Strain.

into a cooled liqueur glass to offer, garnished with a spray of cinnamon and nutmeg.

46. Red Night.

Ingredients.

5 oz water.
3.5 oz raspberry syrup.
0.75 oz Scotch whisky.
0.75 oz interest fruit liqueur.
0.5 oz grenadine 1 orange, juiced.
1.5 oz Prosecco Serves 1.

Instructions

Include water right into raspberry syrup to dilute well before loading an ice.

maker. Put into fridge freezer a few hours to form ice.
Location Scotch whisky, interest fruit liqueur, grenadine, as well as orange juice into a cocktail shaker. Add some raspberry ice cubes. Shake well and also pressure right into a champagne glass. Leading with

Prosecco to offer.

47. Red Rocket.

Ingredients.

1/2 oz peach schnapps.
1/2 oz watermelon schnapps 1/2 oz orange juice.
1 oz vodka.
1/2 oz pineapple juice (optional) 1 dash grenadine.
Serves 1.

Instructions

Shake all ingredients in cocktail shaker well with ice. Strain right into a.

chilled glass to serve.

48. Reindeer Caesar.

Ingredients.

1.5 oz vodka.
6 oz clamato juice 2 tsp lemon juice.
1/4 tsp hot pepper sauce 1 tsp Wocestershire sauce pinch of nutmeg.
sea salt (optional) Serves 1.

Instructions.

Stir all components, except nutmeg, well in a highball glass with ice. Edge.

the glass with lemon juice and sea salt if dream. Garnish with nutmeg to serve.

49. Santa Shot.

Ingredients.

1/3 oz grenadine.
1/3 oz environment-friendly crème de menthe 1/3 oz pepper mint schnapps.
Offers 1.

Instructions

Layer active ingredients as complies with to get the Christmas appearance: grenadine (red),.

crème de menthe (environment-friendly), as well as peppermint schnapps (white).

50. Scotch Holiday Sour.

Ingredients.

0.5 oz wonderful vermouth.
1.5 oz scotch.
1 oz Cherry Marnier or cherry brandy.

1/2 egg white.
1 oz lemon juice lemon slice.
Offers 1.

Instructions

Integrate all components, other than lemon slice. Include ice. Shake in.

cocktail shaker or blend in blender or food processor. Pressure right into a chilled Whiskey Sour glass. Leading with lemon slice to garnish as well as offer.

51. Scroogedriver.

Ingredients.

4 oz orange juice, fresh.
1.5 oz vodka Serves 1.

Instructions

Integrate all components in highball glass with ice to serve.

52. Snowball.

Ingredients.

1/4 oz anisette or Pernod 1/4 oz crème de violette 1/4 oz heavy cream.
1/4 oz white crème de menthe 1 oz Plymouth Gin.
Serves 1.

Instructions.

Incorporate all components with ice in shaker or blender or food processor. Pour into chilled.

champagne glass to offer.

53. Snow Job.

Ingredients.

2 oz pear schnapps.
1 oz whipping cream or half-and-half 1 pinch cinnamon.
Offers 1.

Instructions

Either mix pear schnapps and cream with ice in blender or tremble them.

in cocktail shaker. Pour into glass, leading with ground cinnamon to offer.

54. Tezon Misteltoe.

Ingredients.

1 oz Tequila Tezón Blanco 1/2 oz three-way sec.
1/2 oz fresh pomegranate juice Mumm Champagne pomegranate seeds.
Offers 1.

Instructions.

Prepare a cooled Champagne groove. Gather tequila, triple sec as well as.

pomegranate juice. Fill out with Champagne. Garnish with pomegranate seeds.

55. White Christmas # 1.

Ingredients.

1 oz Scotch whisky.
1 oz White Creme de Cacao 1 oz Creme de Bananes.
1 oz dual cream White chocolate, grated.

Offers 1.

Instructions.

Shake all liqueur components well in a cocktail shaker prior to straining.

into a mixed drink glass. Leading with a spray of grated white delicious chocolate.

56. White Christmas # 2.

Ingredients.

1 oz whipping cream 1 oz vodka.
1oz peppermint schnapps 1 oz white creme de cacao 1 cup ice.
2small candy canes Serves 2.

Instructions.

Shake all liqueur active ingredients in a cocktail shaker with ice cubes.

Pressure.

into chilled glasses and offer with candy cane.

57. White Christmas Dream.

Ingredients.

1 oz vodka.
1 oz amaretto.
1 oz heavy cream nutmeg.
Serves 1.

Instructions.

Shake vodka, amaretto, and also heavy cream well in a cocktail shaker with.

ice. Pressure right into a chilled alcoholic drink glass. Leading with grated nutmeg to offer.

58. White Russian.

Ingredients.

2.5 oz Russian Standard vodka 1 oz coffee liqueur.
1.5 oz fresh cream Serves 1.

Instructions

Pour vodka as well as coffee liqueur into ice-filled glass. Stir delicately. Leading with.

fresh cream.

59. Wintertime Breeze.

Ingredients.

1 oz Creme de Cacao 1 oz vanilla schnapps 1 oz Irish Cream milk.
Offers 1.

Instructions

Put all liqueur components right into a cup, and top with milk. Stir well
to.

offer.

60. Winter months Ice.

Ingredients.

1 oz cream of coconut 2 oz lemonade.
3 oz light whipping cream crushed ice.
1 dashboard cinnamon fresh fruit, chopped.

Offers 1.

Instructions

Area cream of coconut, lemonade, whipping cream, and also smashed ice
in a.

blender. Mix till frothy at high speed as well as pour into glass. Leading
with cinnamon and also fresh fruit.

61. Winter months Sun.

Ingredients.

0.5 oz Cointreau.
0.5 oz vodka.
3.5 oz orange juice 1 oz lime juice.
0.5 oz almond syrup 1 piece orange.
Offers 1.

Instructions

Shake all active ingredients except orange piece in a cocktail shaker with ice.

Pressure right into a highball glass. Garnish with orange piece.

Go Nog Their Socks Off

What will the holidays lack eggnog?
Eggnog is a Christmas classic. Perhaps various other customs connected to the Christmas holidays are amusing and also comforting, yet nothing compares to the scrumptious satisfaction of eggnog. Creamy and scrumptious, it is a group pleaser and a great joyful custom to carry on at parties. While the old-school approach to preparing the classic beverage demands time as well as patience, several still locate it well worth the initiative.
The basic recipe for eggnog remains the exact same: Eggs beaten with sugar, milk, cream and also some sort of spirit. Yet, the variations you can create from this is restricted just by your creativity. Via the years it has developed into a varied mix of versions geared to numerous preferences in addition to requirements. Some provide for specific diets such as the Low Carb Eggnog, and others like the Brandy Eggnog are merely easier to make.
It matters not if you want to develop the typical eggnog or one of lots of more recent adjustments, the dishes here will help to nog the socks off your guests. Satisfied Nogging.

1. Baltimore Eggnog

Ingredients

12 eggs, separated
2 mugs superfine sugar or confectioner's sugar 1 pt cognac
1 mug dark rum
1 mug peach brandy or Madeira 3 pt milk
1 pt cream Grated nutmeg
Offers 28

Guidelines

Whip egg yolks with sugar until thick. Gradually stir in cognac, rum,
peach cream, brandy and milk. Cool up until well cooled.
Beat egg whites in separate bowl till rigid. Transfer egg-yolk combination to a
chilled punch dish. Mix in egg whites gradually without stirring or

beating. Sprinkle nutmeg on top to offer.

2. Bourbon Eggnog

Components

4 huge eggs
6 oz granulated sugar
1tsp freshly-grated nutmeg 1/8 tsp allspice
1/8 tsp clove
1/2 tsp cinnamon
2oz Hennessy VSOP brandy 2 oz Grand Marnier
4 oz Bullleit bourbon 12 oz whole milk
8 oz heavy cream
nutmeg or cinnamon (optional), grated Serves 8

Directions

Mix the eggs for 1 minute with a mixer. Blend in the sugar as well as

seasonings for an additional 30 seconds. Add in the 3 liqueurs slowly and also
mix 30 seconds more. Put in the milk as well as cream to mix for one more 1
minute.
Cover. Best to refrigerate overnight to enable flavors to integrate.
Section 4 oz eggnog in a teacup or sparkling wine flute to serve. Garnish with
nutmeg or cinnamon.

3. Brandy Eggnog

Active ingredients

1.25 oz milk 1 oz brandy
0.5 oz sugar syrup 1 egg yolk
Serves 1

Directions

Shake all ingredients in a cocktail shaker with ice cubes. Ensure to

tremble much more strongly than typical to blend well. Stress into antique glass for offering.
Vary brandy with bourbon, Irish scotch, or rum for various tastes.

4. The golden state Eggnog

Active ingredients

3/4 oz bourbon 3/4 oz brandy 3/4 oz rum
1 oz cream
1 egg Nutmeg
Serves 1

Instructions

Shake all active ingredients well with ice in a cocktail shaker. Pressure right into a.

Collins glass. Leading with nutmeg to offer.

5. Christmas Cheer Eggnog.

Ingredients.

1 oz eggnog.
1/2 oz pepper mint schnapps Serve 1.

Instructions

Layer eggnog first, after that pepper mint schnapps to offer. Mix ingredients together to serve.

6. Cider Nog (Non-alcoholic).

Active ingredients:.
1 egg or egg alternative 1 tbsp sugar.
Apple cider Serves 1.

Instructions

Shake the egg as well as sugar in a cocktail shaker loaded with ice. Pressure into.

an old-fashioned glass. Top up with cooled cider.

7. Coffee Eggnog.

Ingredients.

6 oz milk.
0.5 tsp immediate coffee.
1.5 oz whisky.
1 oz coffee liqueur 1 egg.
1 oz whipping cream 1 tsp sugar syrup ground cinnamon.
Offers 1.

Instructions

Integrate all ingredients, besides cinnamon, in a cocktail shaker or.

blender or food processor with ice. Pressure into cooled Collins glass. Sprinkle ground cinnamon to offer.

8. Easier Than Eggnog.
Components:.
1.5 oz DonQ Anejo Rum.
1.5 oz ruby port.
0.5 oz basic syrup 1 egg.
fresh grated nutmeg Serves 1.

Instructions.

Shake to integrate all components other than nutmeg in a cocktail shaker.

Include ice and tremble well. Stress right into a white wine glass. Sprinkle nutmeg to offer.

9. Easy Eggnog.

Ingredients.

4 mugs half-and-half.
1.5 mugs sugar 12 egg yolks.
0.25 mug bourbon.
0.5 cup brandy.
0.5 cup dark rum.
2 cups heavy cream 1 pt vanilla ice cream grated nutmeg.
Serves 16.

Instructions

Stir to liquify sugar in half-and-half over medium warm in saucepan.

Beat egg yolks in different bowl till frothy, after that slowly mix in some of the warm blend. Transfer back to saucepan and cook over low heat. Mix continuously for around 3 mins till thickens. Put aside to let awesome. Combine in.

bourbon, rum, and also brandy. Cover and cool for 4 hours or more.
Beat whipping cream in a cooled dish till rigid. Fold up into the cooled mixture made earlier. Transfer to punch bowl. Add ice cream. Top with the nutmeg and offer.

10. General Harrison's Eggnog.

Ingredients.

1 egg (whole).
1 mug hard cider.
1 tsp sugar syrup or to taste Serves 1.

Instructions

Blend all components with ice. Pour into a cooled highball glass to offer.

11. Gingerbread Man Eggnog.

Ingredients.

1 oz Goldschläger.
1.5 oz Irish Cream.
1.5 oz Schnapps, butterscotch.
1.5 oz Vodka Eggnog.
Offers 1.

Instructions

Shake all active ingredients except eggnog with ice in a cocktail shaker. Stress.

into tiny snifter glass. Fill glass with eggnog. Stir well before offering.

12.Great-Grandma's Eggnog.

Ingredients.

6 eggs.
1.25 cups white sugar.

1 quart bourbon.
1cup rum.
2quarts half-and-half cream.
2 tsp ground nutmeg, or amount to taste 1 pint heavy light whipping cream.
Serves 32 (4 oz each).

Instructions.

Beat eggs as well as sugar until thick and light. Gradually blend in bourbon, rum,.

half-and-half cream, and nutmeg.
Whip cream in one more chilled bowl till it can stand in a peak, after that fold up right into the egg blend. Put in the refrigerator overnight. Shake well prior

to offering.

13. Hazelnut Eggnog.

Ingredients.

6 eggs, with yolk and white separated 1/3 mug wheel sugar.
3 mugs warm milk.
1 mug hazelnut liqueur (Frangelico) 3/4 cup thickened cream.
Ground nutmeg Serves 8.

Instructions.

Beat egg yolks as well as wheel sugar until creamy and also thick with electrical.

mixer. Mix in hot milk, comply with by liqueur as well as cream before setting aside.
Beat egg whites in a separate dish till soft optimals develop with electric mixer.
Fold up egg whites right into the earlier ready liqueur mix. Pour into glasses and also spray with nutmeg to offer warm or cool.

14. Homemade Eggnog.

Ingredients.

6 eggs, divided.
1/2 mug very fine sugar 1/4 tsp salt.
2 tsp vanilla.
2 cups brandy, rum or scotch 1 mug milk.
nutmeg (usage for garnish additionally) Serves 16.

Instructions

Combine egg yolks, 1/4 mug sugar, vanilla, salt as well as nutmeg together.

Beat up until light and also extremely thick yellow. Blend in the liqueur as well as milk slowly. Cover and cool the combination over night.

Beat the egg whites to soft tops. Gradually assimilate the staying 1/4 cup sugar,
after that defeat to soft tops once again to become a frothy cream.
Carefully fold the cream as well as pour right into the chilled liqueur mix.
Offer in glass or mug with grated nutmeg as topping.

15. Hot Eggnog.

Ingredients.

1 egg Pinch salt.
1tbsp superfine sugar.
1.5 oz brandy 1 cup hot milk Pinch nutmeg.
Offers 1.

Instructions

Beat egg and salt until thick. Blend in sugar. Add brandy and also warm milk;.

mix well. Pour into a heated mug. Leading with ground nutmeg.

16. Low Carb Eggnog.

Ingredients.

1/2 cup Splenda 2 tablespoon Splenda.
2eggs, separated 1/4 tsp salt.
2 cups whipping cream 2 mugs water.
1 tsp vanilla essence.
brandy or rum flavor to preference.
1 tsp eggnog flavored oil (LorAnn or Amish brand name) (optional) 1/2 mug
whipping cream, whipped with sugar of choice ground nutmeg.
Serves 4.

Instructions

Beat egg yolks with 1/2 mug Splenda. Stir in salt, whipping cream, and also.

water. Cook and mix progressively over medium warmth till mixture enlarges.

Deposit to cool.

Beat egg whites in a different dish till frothy. Add in the 2 tbsp Splenda prior to beating more to soft heights.

Mix the egg white mixture completely right into the prepared mixture. Stir in vanilla as well as flavorings. Cool for 4 hours or even more.

Offer in punch dish or mugs, top with whipped cream as well as garnish with nutmeg.

17. Low Fat Eggnog.

Ingredients.

1large egg.

1/4 cup fat-free egg alternative 1/4 mug sugar.

2cups fat-free vaporized milk.

1 tsp vanilla essence.

1/4 mug brandy or rum, 80 proof 1 tsp ground nutmeg.

Offers 4.

Instructions.

Beat the egg, egg replacement as well as sugar together. Mix the combination over.

low heat till it starts to thicken as well as ends up being steamy, however ensuring it is not steaming.

Warm the milk up in separate container until it steams without in fact boiling. Beat the milk gradually right into the egg combination. Mix in the vanilla before enabling the blend to chill extensively.

Mix in the brandy or rum and fill out the glasses. Top with a spray of nutmeg each for serving.

18. Nashville Eggnog.

Ingredients.

1 quart bourbon.

1 pint brandy.
1 pint jamaican rum 18 eggs, separated.
3 quarts heavy cream 2 mugs sugar.
1 entire clove nutmeg.
Offers 25.

Instructions

Mix as well as mix bourbon, brandy, and rum with egg yolks well. Incorporate.

cream as well as sugar to blend into liquor mix. Beat egg whites individually until tight, after that fold slowly right into blend. Garnish with cloves and nutmeg. Serve in little cups.

19.Old-Fashioned Eggnog.

Ingredients.

6 eggs, divided.
1.25 mugs superfine sugar 1 mug dark rum.
1 cup brandy.
0.25 cup bourbon.
1.5 cups heavy cream 1 pint vanilla gelato grated nutmeg.
Offers 12.

Instructions

Beat egg yolks as well as sugar till thick. Beat in the brandy, bourbon as well as rum,.

then the cream.
Beat egg whites in different bowl until soft optimals. Blend into eggnog.
Cover and chill a minimum of 4 hrs.
Transfer combination to punch dish. Place the entire gelato undamaged right into the eggnog. Sprinkle nutmeg ahead to offer.

20. Rum Holiday Eggnog.

Ingredients.

1 big grade AA egg, divided 2 tsp superfine sugar.
1 oz whipping cream.
0.5 tsp pure almond extract.
0.5 tsp pure vanilla extract.
1.5 oz Mount Gay Eclipse Rum Grated cinnamon.
Grated nutmeg Serves 1.

Instructions

Beat the egg yolk in a bowl until rigid. In one more bowl, beat the egg.

white with 1 tsp sugar up until peaks develop. After that gradually fold both the
yolk and also white together.
Beat the cream, almond, vanilla, as well as the remaining 1 tsp sugar in
a different dish till stiff. Fold up the cream combination into the egg
combination gradually. Lastly, add rum and also stir carefully.
Put into refrigerator overnight, or offer instantly over ice. Serve in
a liqueur glass or punch glass, garnished with cinnamon as well as nutmeg.

21. Vegan Eggnog.

Ingredients.

21 oz extra-firm silken tofu 2 mugs soymilk.
2/3 mug turbinado sugar, light brown sugar, or sucanat (or use 1/2 mug honey
or 1 cup alternative liquid sweetener).
1/4 tsp salt.
1 mug cold water.
1 mug rum or brandy.
4 1/2 tsp vanilla essence 20 ice cubes.
nutmeg Serves 10.

Instructions

Blend the tofu and soymilk with the sugar and also salt till very smooth.

Include the brandy, rum or water, as well as vanilla, and also blend them well.
Cover and also place the combination into fridge.
When serving, mix ice right into the combination up until foamy. Pour into
glasses and also serve with nutmeg as topping.

Ingredients

22. White Christmas Nog

- 4 oz eggnog, chilled
- 1/2 oz white chocolate liqueur
- 1 oz Southern Comfort
- edible gold flakes or chocolate flakes

Serves 1

Stir eggnog, white chocolate liqueur, and Southern Comfort in a snifter glass lightly. Top with a sprinkle of flakes to serve.

Get A Kick Out Of A Punch

Punch is a term for a vast bunch of refreshments commonly featuring fruit or fruit juice, and can be alcoholic or non-alcoholic. Ever since the drink was brought in from India to England in early 17th century, the punch has been popular in communal gatherings in the West. A Christmas holiday get-together is no exception.

As the hectic holiday season draws near, planning and organizing a Christmas dinner or party is often very stressful. You can eliminate one of the headaches from the beverage department with the Christmas punch recipes listed below, both alcohol and alcohol-free. They will be a hit with family and friends at your holiday bash. You won't be disappointed.

Now go give them a kick out of a Christmas punch!

1. Angel Punch (Non-Alcoholic)

Ingredients

- 64 oz white grape juice
- 32 oz strong green tea
- 16 oz lemon juice
- 1 cup sugar syrup
- 56 oz club soda

Serves 42 (4 oz each)

Instructions

Combine all ingredients other than the club soda. Put mixture in   fridge till well chilled.

To serve, fill punch bowl with the chilled mixture. Stir in club soda slow and add ice.

2. Apple Cider Punch

Ingredients

- 1 large orange
- 95 oz apple cider
- 30 oz apricot nectar
- 4 oz fresh lemon juice
- 6 sticks cinnamon
- A few whole cloves

Serves 30

Instructions

Stuff the clovers into the orange after cutting holes. Heat the oven at 180°C to bake the orange for around 1/2 hour. Puncture the orange with a fork a few times after taking it out of the oven.

Put all the ingredients, including the orange, into a big pot for boiling with the lid covered. Simmer for 1/2 hour over low heat.

Pour the mixture into a punch bowl for serving. Leave the cinnamon sticks and orange in as decoration or remove them as you wish.

3. Applejack Punch

Ingredients

- 2 bottles (25 oz or 750 ml each) applejack or Calvados
- 2 cups light rum
- 2 cups peach brandy
- 1 cup brandy
- 1 pint lemon juice
- 1/2 cup maple syrup or sugar syrup to taste
- 2 l lemon-lime soda or 1 l each lemon-lime soda and club soda
- 1/2 apple, sliced

Serves 45

Instructions

Pre-chill all **Ingredients.** Mix all ingredients except soda and apple in   a chilled punch bowl well. Add ice block. Stir in soda steadily. Top with apple slices to serve.

4. Berry Christmas Punch

Ingredients

- 1.5 l Ocean Spray raspberry cranberry, well chilled
- 2 x 7 oz Fresita Chilean sparkling wine, well chilled
- 1/2 cup Cointreau
- 2 limes, quartered
- 1 punnet strawberries, washed, halved
- 1 punnet blueberries
- 1 punnet raspberries
- 1/4 cup fresh mint leaves

Serves 6

Instructions

Combine the cranberry juice, sparkling wine and Cointreau into a punch bowl. Squeeze some lime juice into the punch and stir well.

Add the squeezed limes, strawberries, blueberries, raspberries and mint leaves to the punch for serving.

5. Big Party Punch (Non-Alcoholic)

Ingredients

- 12 oz lemon juice
- 8 oz lime juice
- 24 oz orange juice
- 96 oz pineapple juice
- 2 cups sugar
- 1/2 cup mint leaves
- 28 oz club soda
- 56 oz ginger ale
- lemon slices
- orange slices
- 2 cups strawberries halved

Serves 70 (4 oz each)

Instructions

Blend all juices (lemon, lime, orange, and pineapple) in a blender   with sugar. Add mint leaves and put into fridge to chill for at least 2 hours.

When ready to serve, strain into punch bowl over ice cake. Stir in club soda and ginger ale and mix well. Garnish with lemon slices, orange slices, and strawberries.

6. Bubbly Punch

Ingredients

- 6 bottles champagne (or sparkling wine)
- 1/2 bottle (13 oz or 375 ml) brandy
- 2 cups sugar
- 5 lemons, sliced
- 5 limes, sliced
- 5 oranges, sliced
- 1 pineapple (cut into chucks or rings)
- 4 cups strawberries

Serves 35

Instructions

Combine 5 bottles of champagne, brandy, and sugar in a big punch bowl. Mix in thinly sliced lemon, lime, and orange rounds, plus pineapple rings. Stir to mix well.

To serve, garnish with strawberries and top with the last bottle of champagne. Add a block of ice to chill.

7. Champagne Cup Punch

Ingredients

- 4 oz brandy
- 3 oz maraschino liqueur
- 2 oz Benedictine

- 1 l club soda
- 1 bottle (25 oz or 750 ml) champagne
- Orange and lemon slices

Serves 18 (4 oz each)

Put all ingredients, except club soda and champagne, in a punch bowl and let sit. When ready to serve, add and stir in the club soda and champagne. Add a block of ice.

8. Christmas Cranberry Fruit Punch

Ingredients
- 1.5 oz Rum, pineapple
- 0.5 oz Triple Sec
- 3 oz Cranberry Juice
- 1 oz Raspberry Juice

Serves 1

Instructions

Combine and blend ingredients with ice in a cocktail shaker. Strain   into highball glass.

9. Cran-Raspberry Snowball Punch

Ingredients
- 1 bottle (32 oz) Knudsen Cranberry Nectar, chilled
- 1 jar (12 oz) Smucker's Seedless Red Raspberry Jam
- 1.5 bottles (2 l) lemon-lime flavored carbonated beverage, chilled
- 1/2 gallon vanilla or vanilla bean ice cream

Serves 48

Instructions

Blend all ingredients other than the ice cream in a large punch bowl until everything is well mixed. Scoop half of the ice cream to stir into the mixture until frothy. Form 'ice cream snowballs' with the remaining ice cream on top the froth.

10. English Christmas Punch

- 1 large lemon, juiced
- 1 large orange, juiced
- 3 cups strong tea
- 2 bottles (25 oz or 750 ml each) dry red wine
- 1 lb superfine sugar
- 1 bottle (25 oz or 750 ml) dark rum

Serves 27

Cook lemon juice, orange juice, tea, and red wine in a saucepan or chafing dish, making sure not to boil. Pour cooked punch into a punch bowl.

Soak as much sugar completely in rum as possible in a large ladle. Pour remaining sugar into punch bowl. Set the rum in ladle on fire, then pour while flaming into punch. Mix well and put out the flames. Stir the rest of the rum into punch well to serve.

11. Highland Hot Milk Punch

- 2 oz scotch
- 1 tsp sugar syrup or to taste
- 1 oz Drambuie
- 1 eggs (whole), beaten
- 1 cup milk
- Pinch powdered cinnamon

Serves 1

Stir all ingredients other than cinnamon in a saucepan over low heat, making sure not to scorch milk. Pour punch into a warmed mug. Sprinkle cinnamon powder to serve.

12. Holiday Punch #1

- 4 cups cranberry juice cocktail
- 8 cups prepared lemonade
- 2 cups orange juice
- 1 jar (4 oz) maraschino cherries
- 1 bottle (2 l) ginger ale
- 1 orange, sliced in rounds

Serves 40

Mix cranberry juice cocktail, lemonade, and orange juice in a punch bowl before stirring in the maraschino cherries. Put in the fridge for at least 2 hours.

Pour in the ginger ale before serving. Garnish each glass with an orange slice.

13. Holiday Punch #2

- 0.5 cup curaçao
- 4 cups gin, chilled
- 2 oz grenadine
- 1.5 cups lemon juice
- 5 cups orange juice
- 1 l lemon-lime soda
- 4 lemon slices
- 4 orange slices

Serves 32

Combine curaçao, gin, grenadine, lemon juice, and orange juice in a punch bowl. Add a block of ice and stir well. Pour and mix soda in steadily. Garnish with fruit slices to serve.

14. Hot Cranberry Citrus Punch

- 2 quarts cranberry juice cocktail
- 3 cups orange juice
- 1/4 cup white sugar
- 1/4 cup brown sugar
- 2 tbsp fresh lemon juice
- 1 pinch salt
- 2 (3") cinnamon sticks

Serves 20

Mix and stir all ingredients in a slow cooker at least 4 quart large. Make sure the sugar dissolve. Turn the heat high to cook for 4-6 hours. Keep warm at low heat for serving.

15. Hot Wine Punch

- 1 bottle (25 oz) red wine
- 8.5 oz water
- 1 stick cinnamon
- 2 cloves
- 1/2 lemon, thinly sliced
- 3.5 oz sugar

Serves 8

Combine all ingredients in a large saucepan. Stir over low heat   without boiling. Serve warm in mug.

16. Mocha Nog Punch

- 10 parts Kahlúa Mocha
- 5 parts Absolut Vanilla
- 20 parts eggnog

Mix ingredients in a punch bowl. Add an ice block before serving.

17. Mrs. Claus' Wildside Punch

- 25 oz X-Rated Fusion liqueur
- 25 oz Cabo Wabo Blanco Tequila
- 25 oz pomegranate juice
- 25 oz cranberry juice
- lime twists for garnish

Serves 25

Mix all liquid ingredients well in a punch bowl. Scoop into ice filled glass to serve. Top with lime twist to garnish.

18. Singapore Sling Slush

- 4 cups water
- 1/2 cup white sugar
- 1/2 cup grenadine syrup
- 1/2 cup cherry juice

- 1/2 cup lemon juice
- 1/2 cup cherry brandy liqueur
- 2 cups gin
- 2.5 cups pineapple juice
- 1 can (6 oz) frozen pink lemonade concentrate, thawed
- 2 bottles (4 l) lemon-lime flavored carbonated beverage
- 46 maraschino cherries

Serves 46

Instructions

Pour the water into a large container to dissolve the sugar. Stir in all the liquid ingredients except the lemon-lime soda. Refrigerate for 24 hours, stirring 2 times or more in between.

When ready to serve, scoop the slush to fill a glass 1/4 full, then fill up the glass with lemon-lime soda. Top with a cherry to serve.

19. Spiced Percolator Punch

Ingredients

- 1 bottle (64 oz) unsweetened pineapple juice
- 1 bottle (64 oz) cranberry juice cocktail
- 4.5 cups water
- 1 cup brown sugar, packed
- 2 tbsp whole cloves
- 4 (4") cinnamon sticks, broken
- 1/4 tsp salt

Serves 22

Instructions

Fill the coffee percolator up with the liquid **Ingredients.** Put the other ingredients in the basket of the percolator. Prepare the coffee percolator to perk. Serve hot.

Warm And Fuzzy In A Cold Winter

Anybody wants to fight off the winter chill?

Christmas may very well be the time to be jolly, but it is also the time when coldness strikes. Nobody wishes to get out of their cozy beds in the freezing snowy mornings unless there is a reason.

A hot delicious beverage could just be that reason. Traditional warm drinks for the holidays are a good place to begin be it the timeless hot toddy or hot buttered rum. You may also enjoy modern creations like Steaming Swamp or Tom & Jerry.

Give any of the following hot drink recipes compiled a shot in a chilly winter morning. You'll welcome the warm and fuzzy start to another refreshing new day.

Merry Christmas!

1. Adult Hot Chocolate

Ingredients

- 1.5 oz peppermint schnapps
- 1 cup hot chocolate
- 1 tbsp whipped cream

Serves 1

Instructions

Stir peppermint schnapps and hot chocolate in a warmed mug well. Top with whipped cream to serve.

2. Apple Barrel Apres-Ski Toddy

Ingredients

- 1.5 oz apple schnapps
- 1 cup apple cider or apple juice
- 1 oz brandy

- 1 tsp honey or to taste
- Cinnamon stick

Serves 1

Instructions

Heat all ingredients in a saucepan till hot but do not boil. Pour into a hot mug to serve.

3. Down East Hot Buttered Rum

Ingredients

- 1 cup apple cider
- 2 tsp brown sugar
- 4 cloves (whole)
- 1 lemon peel
- 1.5 oz gold rum
- Cinnamon stick
- Grated nutmeg
- Small pat butter

Serves 1

Instructions

Heat apple cider to boiling point. Warm a mug and put sugar in. Stir in a bit of apple cider to dissolve sugar. Add cinnamon, cloves, lemon peel and rum. Fill up with hot apple cider and stir. Top with butter and nutmeg.

4. Flaming Hot Buttered Rum

Ingredients

- 1/2 oz over proof rum
- 1 tbsp brown sugar
- 1 oz dark rum
- Boiling water
- Butter

- Cinnamon stick
- Whole cloves
- Grated nutmeg
- Lemon or orange peel
- Pinch sugar

Serves 1

Warm a large mug. Place in sugar, cinnamon stick, and lemon/orange peel studded with cloves. Pour in some boiling water to dissolve sugar before stirring in rum. Fill the mug up with boiling water and top with pat of butter.

Pour some rum in a ladle with a pinch of sugar. Warm the rum by immersing part of the ladle in hot water. Ignite rum and pour blazing into mug. Add a bit more butter if wish and sprinkle with nutmeg to serve.

5. Holiday Glogg

- 12 oz SKYY vodka
- 1 bottle (25 oz or 750 ml) dry red wine
- 1.5 tbsp mulling spices
- 1 tsp fresh orange zest
- 2 tbsp sugar
- 2 tbsp blanched almonds
- 4 tbsp raisins

Serves 4 (9 oz each)

Use a cheesecloth to wrap the mulling spices. Cook the SKYY vodka, dry red wine, mulling spices (in cheesecloth), orange zest, and sugar in a saucepan. Do not boil, but simmer lightly over medium heat for 1/2 hour or more. Dispose of the mulling spices. Place a few almonds and raisins in each mug, then fill with the hot liquid.

6. Hot Brandy Flip

- 1.5 oz brandy (or rum, whisky or gin may be used)
- 1 egg (whole)
- 1 tsp sugar syrup or to taste
- 2 oz milk (optional)
- Grated nutmeg

Blend brandy, egg, sugar syrup, and (optional) milk. Heat mixture gently in a saucepan. Pour into a warm Delmonico glass. Top with nutmeg.

7. Hot Buttered Rum

- 1.5 oz dark rum
- 1 tsp brown sugar
- 1 tsp butter
- hot milk
- grated nutmeg

Serves 1

Mix dark rum, brown sugar, and butter in mug. Fill with hot milk and stir well. Garnish with nutmeg to serve.

8. Hot Toddy Basic

- generous pinch powdered cinnamon
- 4 whole cloves
- 1.5 oz whiskey or brandy, rum, gin, or vodka
- 1 oz sugar syrup or to taste
- lemon slice

- boiling water
- grated nutmeg
- cinnamon stick

Serves 1

Instructions

Warm an old fashioned glass or a mug. Place powdered cinnamon, cloves, liqueur, sugar syrup, and lemon slice in it. Pour in boiling water and stir. Sprinkle nutmeg and garnish with cinnamon stick.

9. Jersey Flash

Ingredients
- 4 cloves (whole)
- Pinch cinnamon
- Lemon peel
- 1 tsp honey
- 1.5 oz gin
- Hot apple cider
- Grated nutmeg

Serves 1

Instructions

Warm a mug. Put in cloves, cinnamon, lemon peel, and honey. Pour some boiling water to dissolve honey. Add gin and set ablaze for a few seconds. Fill the mug up with hot apple cider. Top up with nutmeg to serve.

10. Mulled Cider

Ingredients
- 4 cloves (whole)
- 1.5 oz gold rum
- 1 cup apple cider or apple juice
- 1 tsp honey or sugar syrup to taste

- Dash Angostura bitters
- Cinnamon stick
- Grated nutmeg
- Pinch ground allspice
- Lemon twist

Serves 1

Heat all ingredients in a saucepan. Strain into a warmed mug to serve.

11. Steaming Swamp

- 1 lime
- fresh mint leaves
- 1/2 tbsp brown sugar
- 2 oz Cachaça
- 3.5 oz boiling water

Serves 1

Cut lime into 8 pieces. Place 6 pieces of lime and some mint leaves in cocktail glass. Mash with wooden pestle, then add sugar.

Heat up cachaça before pouring into glass. Add boiling water and stir well.

Garnish with remaining 2 pieces of lime and mint leaves.

12. Tom & Jerry

- 1 egg, separated
- 1/2 oz simple syrup or 1 tsp powdered sugar
- 1 oz dark rum
- 1 oz Cognac or brandy

- hot milk or hot water
- grated nutmeg

Serves 1

Instructions

Beat egg yoke and egg white separately before folding them together. Pour the mixture into an Irish coffee glass. Put in the simple syrup, dark rum, and brandy. Fill with hot milk and stir well. Top with nutmeg to garnish.